HOLT McDOUGAL LITERATURE

Online Edition
Selection Supplement
British Literature

HOLT McDOUGAL

HOUGHTON MIFFLIN HARCOURT

Printed in the U.S.A.

Typeset in The Sans from LucasFonts.

ART CREDITS

COVER, TITLE PAGE

top left © Dalhousie University Department of Theatre. Halifax, Nova Scotia;
top right © Image Asset Management Ltd./SuperStock;
bottom center © Hulton Archive/Getty Images; *background* © Patrick Ingrand/Getty Images

ISBN 13: 978-0-547-65022-7

3 4 5 6 7 8 9 10 1420 20 19 18 17 16 15 14 13 12 11

4500309788 A B C D E F G

COMMON CORE

TABLE OF CONTENTS

Selected Poetry

by T. S. Eliot

VIDEO TRAILER THINK central KEYWORD: HML12-1116A

COMMON CORE

RL 4 Determine the meaning of words and phrases as they are used in the text, including figurative and connotative meanings; analyze the impact of specific words choices on meaning and tone. **RL 7** Analyze multiple interpretations of a poem, evaluating how each version interprets the source text. **RL 10** Read and comprehend literature, including poems.

DID YOU KNOW?

T. S. Eliot . . .

- refused to publish his early work because he believed it mediocre.
- wrote the book that inspired the hit Broadway musical *Cats.*
- won the Nobel Prize in literature in 1948.

Meet the Author

T. S. Eliot 1888–1965

Claimed by his native America as well as his adopted homeland of Britain, T. S. Eliot was one of the giants of 20th-century literature. With friend and fellow American poet Ezra Pound, Eliot ushered in the modernist movement, transforming how poetry was written and understood.

Poet of Two Countries Thomas Stearns Eliot was born in St. Louis, Missouri, into a distinguished family with New England roots. Eliot's parents maintained close ties to New England, bringing their children each summer to Gloucester, Massachusetts. Later, Eliot remarked that as a child he did not feel as if he truly belonged in either New England or the Midwest.

After attending Harvard University, Eliot pursued graduate work in philosophy at the Sorbonne in Paris, at Harvard, and at Oxford University. However, he never earned his doctoral degree. In 1915, he fell in love with a vivacious English beauty named Vivien Haigh-Wood. He married Vivien just a few months later, much to the consternation of his parents, who were deeply troubled by her history of mental illness. Henceforth, Eliot would make his home in England.

Breaking with the Past A quiet, cultured man, Eliot supported himself and his wife by working successively as a teacher, a bank clerk, and an editor while trying to make a name for himself as a writer. In 1917, with Ezra Pound's support, Eliot published a collection of poems, *Prufrock and Other Observations,* which explored the alienating effects of modern life. Though now considered a cornerstone of the modernist movement, the volume received mixed reviews when it first appeared. Many critics were put off by Eliot's vivid depictions of the ugly realities of urban life and by his use of fragmentary images and colloquial language.

Modernist Master With the publication of *The Waste Land* in 1922, Eliot's reputation as a pre-eminent poet was solidified. Completed as his marriage was falling apart, the poem expresses the emotional pain and spiritual emptiness felt by the post–World War I generation and by Eliot himself. Yearning for spiritual comfort and meaning, Eliot joined the Church of England in 1927. In his later poems, such as "Ash Wednesday" (1930) and *Four Quartets* (1943), Eliot stressed the importance of religious belief to leading a purposeful life. When the legendary poet died in 1965, his friend and editor Robert Giroux wrote, "the world became a lesser place."

Author Online THINK central

Go to thinkcentral.com. KEYWORD: HML12-1116B

TEXT ANALYSIS: STYLE

Credited with ushering in a new era of poetry, T. S. Eliot shattered the poetic conventions of his day. Eliot's revolutionary **style**—his individual way of communicating ideas—has inspired both praise and puzzlement for almost a century. Key elements of Eliot's poetic style include

- a frequent use of free verse, in which the rhythms fall into no fixed pattern
- the use of colloquial language, including slang and references to popular culture
- the conveying of ideas by complex figurative language, images, symbols, and allusions rather than by explicit statements

Eliot's tone is another important element of his style. Many of his poems have a tone of disillusionment or alienation, reflecting his despair at what he saw as the decline of Western civilization. "The Naming of Cats," written after Eliot came to terms with the modern age, shows the poet's witty, whimsical side.

As you read Eliot's poetry, notice examples of these stylistic elements.

READING STRATEGY: READING MODERN VERSE

Eliot's modernist poetry, like much modern art, can be hard to understand at first. Eliot often presents a patchwork of images, symbols, and allusions; readers must supply the connections themselves. The following guidelines can help you interpret Eliot's poems:

- Read each poem aloud, pausing between sections and lingering over images you find particularly striking.
- Try paraphrasing lines you find puzzling.
- Use the sidenotes to decipher unfamiliar allusions.

For "Preludes" and "The Hollow Men," use a chart like the one shown to jot down the central image or idea conveyed in each stanza.

Poem / Stanza	Central Image or Idea
"Preludes," stanza 1	The speaker describes a lonely, rundown, working-class setting—this modern environment is terribly bleak.

Complete the activities in your **Reader/Writer Notebook**.

Is the world FALLING APART?

Once in a while, an event takes place that makes people feel as if their world is in danger of disintegration. For T. S. Eliot and his contemporaries, World War I was an event of this kind. One of the bloodiest conflicts of all time, the war seemed to them a total breakdown of Western civilization. In two of the poems that follow, Eliot conveys the alienation and despair that people felt in the wake of this catastrophe.

QUICKWRITE Think about events—such as wars, terrorist attacks, or natural disasters—that have shaken entire nations. Choose one event and describe how it altered the lives of those affected. What changes in values or perceptions does such an act cause? How might it make people fear society's disintegration?

Preludes

T. S. Eliot

I

The winter evening settles down
With smell of steaks in passageways.
Six o'clock.
The burnt-out ends of smoky days.
And now a gusty shower wraps
The grimy scraps
Of withered leaves about your feet
And newspapers from vacant lots;
The showers beat
On broken blinds and chimney-pots,
And at the corner of the street
A lonely cab-horse steams and stamps.
And then the lighting of the lamps. **A**

II

The morning comes to consciousness
Of faint stale smells of beer
From the sawdust-trampled street
With all its muddy feet that press
To early coffee-stands.
With the other masquerades
That time resumes,
One thinks of all the hands
That are raising dingy shades
In a thousand furnished rooms.

III

You tossed a blanket from the bed,
You lay upon your back, and waited;
You dozed, and watched the night revealing
The thousand sordid images
Of which your soul was constituted;
They flickered against the ceiling.

2 steaks: here, cheap cuts from low-grade beef, once a common working-class food.

A READING MODERN VERSE
Which images in the first stanza create the most vivid impression? Explain why.

18 early coffee-stands: stands of vendors who cater to early-morning pedestrians.

23 furnished rooms: one-room apartments with furniture included, usually cheap and rundown.

And when all the world came back
And the light crept up between the shutters
And you heard the sparrows in the gutters,
You had such a vision of the street
As the street hardly understands;
Sitting along the bed's edge, where
You curled the papers from your hair,
Or clasped the yellow soles of feet
In the palms of both soiled hands.

36 curled . . . hair: removed the paper curlers around which hair was wound; suggests that the "you" being addressed is a woman.

IV

His soul stretched tight across the skies
That fade behind a city block,
Or trampled by insistent feet
At four and five and six o'clock;
And short square fingers stuffing pipes,
And evening newspapers, and eyes
Assured of certain certainties,
The conscience of a blackened street
Impatient to assume the world. **B**

B STYLE
"His" in line 39 refers to the street. In lines 39–47, Eliot **personifies** the street, just as morning is personified in Section II. Why do you think Eliot employs this stylistic technique? Explain what you think it serves to convey or emphasize.

I am moved by fancies that are curled
Around these images, and cling:
The notion of some infinitely gentle
Infinitely suffering thing.

Wipe your hand across your mouth, and laugh;
The worlds revolve like ancient women
Gathering fuel in vacant lots.

Text Analysis

1. **Summarize** Describe the poem's **setting,** citing specific lines or phrases that allow you to envision the place Eliot describes.
2. **Interpret** A prelude is a short musical piece based on a recurrent theme. Why do you think Eliot titled this poem "Preludes"? Does knowing the meaning of this word give you any new insights into the poem? Explain.

The Hollow Men

T. S. Eliot

Mistah Kurtz—he dead.
A penny for the Old Guy

[Epigraph] Mistah . . . dead: a quotation from Joseph Conrad's *Heart of Darkness,* in which Kurtz is a character whose descent into evil makes him like the "lost violent souls" in lines 15–16. **A penny . . . Guy:** a cry used by English children collecting money to buy fireworks for Guy Fawkes Day, a yearly celebration of the failure of Guy Fawkes and other conspirators to blow up Parliament in 1605. The celebration also traditionally includes the burning of straw effigies of Fawkes.

4 Headpiece . . . straw: The speaker likens himself and the other "hollow men" to the straw effigies burned on Guy Fawkes Day.

I

We are the hollow men
We are the stuffed men
Leaning together
Headpiece filled with straw. Alas!
Our dried voices, when
We whisper together
Are quiet and meaningless
As wind in dry grass
Or rats' feet over broken glass
In our dry cellar

Shape without form, shade without colour,
Paralysed force, gesture without motion;

Those who have crossed
With direct eyes, to death's other Kingdom
Remember us—if at all—not as lost
Violent souls, but only
As the hollow men
The stuffed men. (C)

14 death's other Kingdom: perhaps heaven (as opposed to hell, where the "lost violent souls" go).

(C) STYLE
Recall that Eliot often conveys ideas through **symbols** and **allusions** instead of direct statements. Why does the speaker liken himself and his companions to straw effigies?

II

Eyes I dare not meet in dreams
In death's dream kingdom
These do not appear:
There, the eyes are
Sunlight on a broken column
There, is a tree swinging
And voices are
In the wind's singing
More distant and more solemn
Than a fading star.

Let me be no nearer
In death's dream kingdom
Let me also wear
Such deliberate disguises
Rat's coat, crowskin, crossed staves
In a field
Behaving as the wind behaves
No nearer—

Not that final meeting
In the twilight kingdom

33 Rat's coat . . . field: a typical scarecrow with small animals attached. The staves are the poles that support it.

III

This is the dead land
This is cactus land
Here the stone images
Are raised, here they receive
The supplication of a dead man's hand
Under the twinkle of a fading star.

Is it like this
In death's other kingdom
Waking alone
At the hour when we are
Trembling with tenderness
Lips that would kiss
Form prayers to broken stone. D

43 supplication (sŭp′lĭ-kā′shən): begging; plea.

D READING MODERN VERSE
Note the different **images** Eliot presents of the "dead land." What does each image convey? Together, what do they tell you about the hollow men's existence?

IV

The eyes are not here
There are no eyes here
In this valley of dying stars
In this hollow valley
This broken jaw of our lost kingdoms

In this last of meeting places
We grope together
And avoid speech
Gathered on this beach of the tumid river

Sightless, unless
The eyes reappear
As the perpetual star
Multifoliate rose
Of death's twilight kingdom
The hope only
Of empty men.

60 tumid (to͞o′mĭd): swollen.

64 Multifoliate (mŭl′tə-fō′lē-āt′) **rose:** an allusion to the many-petaled rose formed by the souls of the blessed in Dante's *Divine Comedy.*

V

Here we go round the prickly pear
Prickly pear prickly pear
Here we go round the prickly pear
At five o'clock in the morning.

68–71 ***Here . . . morning:*** a variation of the children's rhyme "Here We Go 'Round the Mulberry Bush," replacing the mulberry bush with a prickly pear cactus, appropriate to the "cactus land" of line 40.

Between the idea
And the reality
Between the motion
And the act
Falls the Shadow
For Thine is the Kingdom E
Between the conception
And the creation
Between the emotion
And the response
Falls the Shadow
Life is very long
Between the desire
And the spasm
Between the potency
And the existence
Between the essence
And the descent
Falls the Shadow F
For Thine is the Kingdom
For Thine is
Life is
For Thine is the

This is the way the world ends
This is the way the world ends
This is the way the world ends
Not with a bang but a whimper.

E ALLUSION
An **allusion** is an indirect reference to a person, place, event, or literary work with which the author believes the reader will be familiar. Here Eliot is quoting the beginning of a sentence added to the Lord's Prayer by many Christians. The "Kingdom" to which it refers is the kingdom of God. If this appears to be the speech of the Hollow Men, why might they repeat this line from the Lord's Prayer?

F STYLE
How do you interpret the "Shadow" mentioned here and in lines 76 and 82? Explain what you think it might **symbolize.**

COMMON CORE RL 7

READING MODERN VERSE
Eliot's style and tone invite a range of interpretations. Search an Internet video site using the terms "hollow men" and "eliot" to view more than one interpretation. How are they similar and different from one another and from your own interpretation of this poem?

Text Analysis

1. **Summarize** Describe the hollow men. What are their key **traits,** and what is their existence like?
2. **Analyze Imagery** What images are repeated in this poem? What ideas do these images convey? Cite evidence to support your answer.

from The Book of Practical Cats

The Naming of Cats

T. S. Eliot

The Naming of Cats is a difficult matter,
It isn't just one of your holiday games;
You may think at first I'm as mad as a hatter
When I tell you, a cat must have THREE DIFFERENT NAMES.
First of all, there's the name that the family use daily,
Such as Peter, Augustus, Alonzo or James,
Such as Victor or Jonathan, George or Bill Bailey—
All of them sensible everyday names.
There are fancier names if you think they sound sweeter,
Some for the gentlemen, some for the dames:
Such as Plato, Admetus, Electra, Demeter—
But all of them sensible everyday names.
But I tell you, a cat needs a name that's particular,
A name that's peculiar, and more dignified,
Else how can he keep up his tail perpendicular,
Or spread out his whiskers, or cherish his pride?
Of names of this kind, I can give you a quorum,
Such as Munkustrap, Quaxo, or Coricopat,
Such as Bombalurina, or else Jellylorum—
Names that never belong to more than one cat.
But above and beyond there's still one name left over,
And that is the name that you never will guess;
The name that no human research can discover—
But the CAT HIMSELF KNOWS, and will never confess. G
When you notice a cat in profound meditation,
The reason, I tell you, is always the same:
His mind is engaged in a rapt contemplation
Of the thought, of the thought, of the thought of his name:
His ineffable effable
Effanineffable
Deep and inscrutable singular Name.

11 Plato . . . Demeter: names from classical Greek and Roman times.

17 quorum (kwôr′əm): a select group or company.

G STYLE
How does this poem differ stylistically from the two preceding ones? Do you see any similarities? Explain, citing evidence.

29 ineffable (ĭn-ĕf′ə-bəl): too awesome or sacred to be spoken; **effable** (ĕf′ə-bəl): capable of being uttered.

Comprehension

COMMON CORE

RL 1 Cite evidence to support inferences drawn from the text. **RL 2** Determine two or more themes or central ideas of a text. **RL 4** Determine the meaning of words and phrases as they are used in the text, including figurative and connotative meanings; analyze the impact of specific word choices on meaning and tone. **RL 10** Read and comprehend literature, including poems.

1. **Recall** According to "The Naming of Cats," how many names must a cat have?
2. **Clarify** What are the different uses of the names?

Text Analysis

3. **Understand Modern Verse** Review the images and ideas you recorded as you read "Preludes." What view of modern urban life does Eliot convey through each of the following?
   - description of the storm (lines 5–13)
   - portrayal of morning (lines 14–23)
   - depiction of the street (lines 39–47)
   - final simile (lines 53–54)
4. **Draw Conclusions** How do you interpret Section V of "The Hollow Men"? What do you think keeps the hollow men from fulfillment? Support your conclusions with textual evidence.
5. **Analyze Sound Devices** Eliot often uses sound devices to connect his fragmentary images. Re-examine "The Hollow Men," noting examples of each sound device listed in the chart. Use your completed chart to describe the effect these sound devices have on the poem.

Sound Device	Example
rhyme	
alliteration	
consonance	

6. **Analyze Mood** The **imagery** in a poem usually contributes to its mood. How would you describe the mood of "Preludes" and that of "The Hollow Men"? How does the mood of "The Naming of Cats" differ?
7. **Examine Style** Re-examine "Preludes" and "The Hollow Men," noting examples of the stylistic elements discussed on page 1117. What relationship do you see between Eliot's style and his message? Do you think his style mirrors his ideas about the human condition? Cite evidence.

Text Criticism

8. **Critical Interpretations** Eliot has always been both praised and criticized. One of his detractors bemoaned the "sterility, inaction, detachment, and despair which dominate Eliot's poetry." Do you agree with this assessment of Eliot's work? Explain, citing evidence from the text.

Is the world FALLING APART?

"Preludes" and "The Hollow Men" are concerned with the disintegration of traditional values and beliefs in the modern world. What works of literature or films that you know of deal with this topic in today's culture?

Language

GRAMMAR AND STYLE: Choose Effective Words

One of the striking aspects of Eliot's poetic style is his use of highly **effective words.** In "Preludes," for example, he uses fresh, evocative **adjectives** to create a disturbing image of an urban wasteland. Note how, in this passage, the adjectives work to create the atmosphere of desolation that Eliot wants to convey to the reader:

And now a gusty shower wraps
The grimy scraps
Of withered leaves about your feet
And newspapers from vacant lots; (lines 5–8)

PRACTICE Review the following stanza. Then, mimicking Eliot's poetic style, replace the adjectives in the stanza with more vivid ones that better convey an atmosphere of decay and destitution.

The rain poured down
On old gutters full of old leaves and faded trash
And in the dark doorway of an unoccupied cafe
A man clasped his thin knees
To his skinny chest

COMMON CORE

L 3 Apply knowledge of language to make effective choices for meaning and style. **W 3d** Use precise words and phrases to convey a vivid picture of the events, setting, and/or characters.

READING-WRITING CONNECTION

YOUR TURN

Expand your understanding of Eliot's style by responding to this prompt. Then use the **revising tips** to improve your poem.

WRITING PROMPT	REVISING TIPS
COMPOSE A POEM Review lines 39–47 of "Preludes," carefully considering Eliot's personification of the street. Adopting the identity of the street itself, write a **three-to-five-stanza poem** that presents some of the images the street "sees" during the long night. Try to imitate Eliot's style by creating a patchwork of images, symbols, and allusions.	• Add more literary allusions or quotations if your poem does not seem to match Eliot's style. • Make sure your poem includes some examples of sound devices such as alliteration, consonance, or assonance (see page 840).

Interactive Revision
THINK central
Go to thinkcentral.com.
KEYWORD: HML12-1125

Telephone Conversation

Poem by Wole Soyinka

COMMON CORE

RL 4 Analyze the impact of specific word choices on meaning and tone. **RL 6** Analyze a case in which grasping point of view requires distinguishing what is directly stated in a text from what is really meant. **RL 10** Read and comprehend literature, including poems.

DID YOU KNOW?

Wole Soyinka . . .

- was the first African to win the Nobel Prize in literature.
- is the cousin of Nigerian music star Fela Kuti.
- spent time working with inner-city kids in Jamaica.

Meet the Author

Wole Soyinka born 1934

Although Wole Soyinka (wō′lĕ shô-yĭng′kə) may be best known for his challenging plays, he is also a distinguished poet and a passionate political activist. He has been arrested at least ten times for his outspoken criticism of government corruption in his native Nigeria. His activist impulses also inform his creative work, which often tackles difficult social issues through blistering satire. Soyinka's resolute advocacy, in art and in practical politics, has earned him the reputation as "the conscience of Nigeria."

Origins Soyinka grew up in an Anglican mission compound in western Nigeria, which was then under British colonial rule. He describes his childhood home as a place "where words were an integral part of culture." Soyinka's family were Yoruba, members of one of Nigeria's main ethnic or tribal groups. Soyinka's grandfather introduced him to Yoruban folklore, including legends of the god Ogun, who governed both the creative and destructive essence. Soyinka frequently invokes Ogun in his work and considers this figure to be his muse.

An African Abroad In late 1954, Soyinka left Nigeria for England, to study at the University of Leeds. After graduating in 1957, he worked as a script reader, actor, and director for London's Royal Court Theater. He also began to write his first serious plays. *The Invention,* the first of Soyinka's plays to be produced, is a satire about the chaos that ensues when black South Africans lose their pigment and can no longer be distinguished from whites.

During his years in England, Soyinka had many personal encounters with the indignities of racism. He satirized one such encounter in his poem "Telephone Conversation," written in 1960. That same year, Nigeria gained its independence from Britain and Soyinka returned to his homeland to study West African drama at the University of Ibadan.

Hybrid Style As Soyinka matured, he became more aware of the tension between traditional African identity and Western-style modernization. He attempts to resolve this in his dramatic work by using a blend of traditional Yoruban folk-drama and European theatrical forms. His major works include *A Dance of the Forests* (1960) and *Death and the King's Horseman* (1976). He has described his writing as "preoccupied with the theme of the oppressive boot, the irrelevance of the color of the foot that wears it and the struggle for individuality."

Author Online THINK central

Go to thinkcentral.com. KEYWORD: HML12-1332

TEXT ANALYSIS: TONE IN SATIRE

As you've learned, **satire** is a literary form in which flaws in human behavior or social institutions are ridiculed in order to promote social change. Because the satirist relies on wit and humor to make a point, his or her **tone,** or attitude toward the subject, is a critical element in this kind of writing. Consider these lines from Soyinka's poem:

"ARE YOU DARK? OR VERY LIGHT?" Revelation came.
"You mean—like plain or milk chocolate?"

The comparison of skin color to varieties of chocolate highlights the absurdity of racial prejudice.

Writers choose words and details carefully to establish tone, which can range from light and humorous to sarcastic and bitter. In fact, the two main types of satire are defined primarily by differences in tone. In **Horatian satire,** the tone is playful and amusing, whereas in **Juvenalian satire,** the tone is biting and harsh. As you read Soyinka's poem, note how his tone helps to deliver his message.

READING SKILL: UNDERSTAND AUTHOR'S BACKGROUND

To understand why someone wrote a particular work, it can be helpful to examine the **author's background.** Background includes not only biographical details but also the values, traditions, and beliefs that have influenced the author's outlook. Before reading "Telephone Conversation," reread the biography of Soyinka on page 1332. Then, as you read the poem, consider how Soyinka's life experiences might have influenced his choice of subject.

Complete the activities in your **Reader/Writer Notebook**.

What causes RACISM?

Most societies have had to confront the problem of racism. But how does racism develop? Are people born with an instinct for prejudice, or do they learn these attitudes from the world around them? What causes a person to feel contempt for another on the basis of race?

QUICKWRITE Consider several possible causes of racism, such as human instinct, fear, ignorance, or hatred. What do you think causes racism? Is it a problem that can be solved? Write a paragraph briefly explaining your position.

Telephone Conversation

Wole Soyinka

The price seemed reasonable, location
Indifferent. The landlady swore she lived
Off premises. Nothing remained
But self-confession. "Madam," I warned,
"I hate a wasted journey—I am African." **A**
Silence. Silenced transmission of
Pressurized good-breeding. Voice, when it came,
Lipstick-coated, long gold-rolled
Cigarette-holder pipped. Caught I was, foully.

"HOW DARK?" . . . I had not misheard . . . "ARE YOU LIGHT
"OR VERY DARK?" Button B. Button A. Stench
Of rancid breath of public hide-and-speak.
Red booth. Red pillar-box. Red double-tiered
Omnibus squelching tar. It *was* real! Shamed
By ill-mannered silence, surrender
Pushed dumbfoundment to beg simplification.
Considerate she was, varying the emphasis—

A AUTHOR'S BACKGROUND
Reread lines 1–5. What aspects of Soyinka's biography are reflected in the speaker's situation?

13 **pillar-box:** mailbox on a pillar.

Language Coach

Etymology Words formed from another word or base are derivations. Look up the word *dumbfoundment* (line 16). What words are at its base? What does it mean? How can it "beg simplification"?

Q.E.H. (1998), Anne Desmet. Wood engraving and linocut, 10.2 cm × 13.3 cm. Private collection. © Bridgeman Art Library.

THE QUEEN
HOSPITAL FOR

"ARE YOU DARK? OR VERY LIGHT?" Revelation
came.
"You mean—like plain or milk chocolate?"
Her assent was clinical, crushing in its light
Impersonality. Rapidly, wave-length adjusted,
I chose, "West African sepia"—and as an afterthought,
"Down in my passport." Silence for spectroscopic
Flight of fancy, till truthfulness clanged her accent
Hard on the mouthpiece "WHAT'S THAT?", conceding,
"DON'T KNOW WHAT THAT IS." "Like brunette."

"THAT'S DARK, ISN'T IT?" "Not altogether.
"Facially, I am brunette, but madam, you should see
"The rest of me. Palm of my hand, soles of my feet
"Are a peroxide blonde. Friction, caused—
"Foolishly, madam—by sitting down, has turned
"My bottom raven black.—One moment madam!"—
sensing
Her receiver rearing on the thunder clap
About my ears—"Madam," I pleaded, "wouldn't you rather
"See for yourself?" B

22 sepia (sē'pē-ə): a dark yellow brown or olive brown.

23 spectroscopic: pertaining to the analysis of colors.

B TONE IN SATIRE
What is absurd about the conversation in this stanza? What in Soyinka's **word choice** helps convey this absurdity?

Comprehension

1. **Recall** What is the speaker's situation at the start of the poem?
2. **Clarify** Why does he reveal that he is African?
3. **Summarize** Reread lines 27–32. What is the speaker's response to the landlady's question?

Text Analysis

4. **Make Inferences About Speaker** Compare the speaker's emotional state at the beginning and the end of the poem. How has the conversation affected him?
5. **Examine Author's Background** What personal experiences, values, or beliefs seem to have inspired Soyinka to write this poem? Cite details from the author's biography and the poem in your answer.
6. **Identify Tone in Satire** Describe the tone of this poem. What specific word choices contribute to this tone? How does the tone affect the way you read the poem? Explain your answer.
7. **Analyze Irony** Satirists frequently use **verbal irony,** which occurs when what is said is the opposite of what is meant. Explain the verbal irony in each of the following passages:
   - the speaker's initial reaction (lines 14–16)
   - the landlady's second question (line 18)
   - the speaker's self-description (lines 30–32)
8. **Make Generalizations** Consider what the landlady's concern with the speaker's precise color suggests about the nature of her racism. What does her reaction tell you about how some people adopt and apply racist beliefs?
9. **Compare Texts** Compare Soyinka's poem with Jonathan Swift's "A Modest Proposal" on page 622. What do these two satires have in common? In what ways are they different? In your answer, compare the following elements:
   - tone
   - type of satire
   - author's style
   - the issue being satirized

Text Criticism

10. **Critical Interpretations** South African writer Nadine Gordimer has described Soyinka's work as "overly self-conscious." Based on the poem you read, do you agree or disagree? Explain, citing details to support your answer.

What causes RACISM?

What do you think Soyinka believes to be the cause of racism? Explain why you agree or disagree with him.

COMMON CORE

RL 1 Cite textual evidence to support inferences drawn from the text. **RL 4** Analyze the impact of specific word choices on meaning and tone. **RL 6** Analyze a case in which grasping point of view requires distinguishing what is directly stated in a text from what is really meant. **RL 10** Read and comprehend literature, including poems.

ACKNOWLEDGMENTS

Houghton Mifflin Harcourt and Faber and Faber Limited: "The Hollow Men" from *Collected Poems* 1909–1962 by T. S. Eliot. Copyright © 1936 by Harcourt Brace & Company, copyright © 1964, 1963 by T. S. Eliot. Reprinted by permission of Houghton Mifflin Harcourt Publishing Company and Faber and Faber Limited.

"The Naming of Cats" from *Old Possum's Book of Practical Cats* by T. S. Eliot. Copyright © 1939 by T. S. Eliot and renewed 1967 © by Esme Valerie Eliot. Reprinted by permission of Houghton Mifflin Harcourt Publishing Company and Faber and Faber Limited.

Melanie Jackson Agency: "Telephone Conversation," by Wole Soyinka. Copyright © 1962, 1990 by Wole Soyinka. Reprinted with permission of the Melanie Jackson Agency, LLC .

ART CREDITS

1116 *left* © Bettmann/Corbis; *background* © Altrendo Panoramic/Getty Images; **1117** © Stephan Agostini/AFP/Getty Images; 1332 *foreground* © Wyman Ira/Corbis Sygma; *background* © Marilyn Kingwill/ArenaPAL/Topham/The Image Works, Inc.; **1333** *foreground, background* © Getty Images; **1335** *Q.E.H.* (1998), Anne Desmet. Wood engraving and linocut, 10.2 cm x 13.3 cm. Private collection. © Bridgeman Art Library.